Barking
The Sound of a
Language

Turid Rugaas

Dogwise™ Publishing
Wenatchee, Washington U.S.A.

Barking
The Sound of a Language
Turid Rugaas

Dogwise Publishing
A Division of Direct Book Service, Inc.
403 South Mission Street, Wenatchee, Washington 98801
1-509-663-9115, 1-800-776-2665
www.dogwisepublishing.com / info@dogwisepublishing.com

© 2008 Turid Rugaas

Graphic Design: Nathan Woodward & Lindsay Peternell

Library of Congress Cataloging-in-Publication Data

Rugaas, Turid.
  Barking : the sound of a language / by Turid Rugaas.
    p. cm.
  ISBN-13: 978-1-929242-51-1 (alk. paper)
  1. Dogs--Barking. I. Title.
  SF433.R84 2008
  636.7'0887--dc22
                                    2007051580
ISBN 978-1-929242-51-1
Printed in the U.S.A.

Contents

1 Barking as Communication

When the topic of barking comes up, people often first think that:

- A dog is showing aggressive behavior

- The dog is dominant

- Dogs do it to irritate us

- It is bad behavior on the part of the dog

- It is a cause of complaint from neighbors

On a superficial basis, these reactions make sense. Nothing is more irritating to people than barking. It makes many people very angry and gets on their nerves and neighbors often complain. People often respond to barking by becoming irritable, angry, nervous, and unsure about what the dog is doing.

Such reactions are based on a lack of knowledge about why dogs bark—and people tend to over-react to what they do not understand. Typical responses include yelling and wanting to punish the dog—all of which usually have the opposite effect from what was intended. Instead of quieting the dog, it often results in just more barking. If it does succeed in quieting the dog, there are usually negative side effects. The dog will likely become afraid of the owner (or neighbor), more afraid of being alone, or develop eating or health problems. A whole range of symptoms due to chronic stress may develop in the dog.

These types of reactions to barking are the result of not understanding what is really going on when a dog barks. Knowledge provides understanding, and understanding gives us a little more insight and patience. When we are not stressed ourselves, we become able to keep a cool head, and self-control lets us handle problems better. We become better observers and can find smarter and more efficient solutions to the problems we face. In other words, analyzing the situation and calmly finding the reasons for what is happening is the best way to find a lasting and good solution without scaring or mentally destroying the dog.

Barking as Communication

Barking and the use of body language are important means by which dogs communicate. Vocal sounds and body language are used by all sorts of animals and people to express a wide variety of needs and emotions. Communication is necessary to be able to live together in a relationship with minimal conflicts and to be able to understand each other well. The key to understanding how to interact with a barking dog is learning how to interpret what a dog is trying to communicate.

This concept applies to humans as well as to dogs. In books and articles about family therapy it is often stated that most of the problems families struggle with arise due to a lack of ability to communicate—to talk with each other. They talk past each other, and accuse each other of "not listening to what I say." "You never listen to me" is a common accusation, often yelled at the top of the voice, and the yelling becomes louder and louder the more people do not feel they are being listened to.

It is exactly the same with dogs. When we think a dog is not listening, we yell louder and more angrily. Dogs also get frustrated about "not being heard." They start "yelling" also—especially when no matter how much they bark, they fail to make us understand what they are trying to communicate.

It is important for us to teach ourselves to "listen" to what our dogs try to tell us. Ideally we can recognize their attempts to communicate—the calming signals, the small signs of stress—so we can solve problems before there is a real conflict. We need to pick up on the communication as early as possible. Or, if conflict has occurred, and we already feel we have a problem, to start "listening" more intently to what the dog is actually telling us. It is only then we can find the right means to solve the problem in a good way.

We must learn to listen to what the dog is telling us.

Most mammals use a variety of sounds and body language to communicate.

So How Do Dogs Try To Communicate?

Dogs have many different ways of expressing themselves beyond barking. Most (but not all) dogs communicate in a similar manner and these expressions can usually be easily recognized by other dogs. Some forms of communication are easy for people to understand, but some unique expressions are harder for people to comprehend without taking the time to learn about them. Dogs communicate in many ways including:

- Distance creating signals used to keep someone away or increase the distance from another individual. Examples are showing teeth, lunging forward, snapping, biting, growling, and barking.

- Calming signals used to express politeness, solve conflicts, or to show friendliness.

- Body language that express fear or defense. Examples are tail between the legs, crouching, backing up or taking flight, and of course the stress symptoms like peeing, scratching, and shaking.

- Signs of joy. Examples are a wagging tail, licking, jumping, wiggling the whole body, and showing a happy face.

And then there are all the sounds that dogs make including:

- Barking

- Whining

- Growling

- Howling

All of these are a natural part of what we can call the language of dogs. They are intended to communicate something to the world around them, and to express the feelings the dog has at that moment. Gaining a better understanding of what a dog is trying to communicate and why he may be trying to communicate when he barks will be the focus of the remainder of this book.

2 When Barking is a Problem

Barking is a natural way for dogs to express themselves—it is a part of their language. Nobody would ever dream about "training away" or "punishing away" a cat that meows or a horse that whinnies. But many people believe that dogs should not be allowed to bark or growl.

First and foremost you must understand and accept that dogs actually have a language, and that a part of that language is to make sounds. It is as simple as that. But given that, it must be admitted that vocal expressions in dogs can have formidable dimensions, and can be a problem for their surroundings including the people nearby.

The key to finding a solution to this is to learn to recognize the point at which barking has become exaggerated because of a need for attention, stress, or has developed into "yelling" because nobody listened when the dog tried to communicate in a more normal way. It can happen in an isolated situation or it can be chronic. But in either case, when there is stress involved, it often comes out through the mouth—not unlike people!

No matter what the cause is, you can do something about it. You have to find the reason for the problem, what kind of barking you are confronted with, and understand the circumstances around it. Then you can identify ways to minimize the barking, remove whatever caused it, and in that way, get control of the problem.

The aim should not be to stop all barking for good. You should not be trying to take away from dogs the language they naturally have. The goal should be to get it down to a level and intensity that you can live with and that permits the dog to act in a way that is natural to him. And, of course, you need to look at your own reactions to a particular barking event since you may be over-reacting.

Keeping Records

If you are experiencing problem barking with your dog, it is useful to start detailed records of the dog's barking behavior. This will allow you to know when your dog barks, what causes the barking, and what actions the dog takes in addition to barking. As you will see in later chapters, having this information will allow you to determine what training and management strategies to adopt to deal with problem barking.

Every time the dog is barking, make notations (see the form on page 14) of exactly how long the dog barks, what situation the dog is in, what he is barking at, etc.

My dog trainer students are asked to carry out a barking study as part of their education, and many of them are really surprised by the results. Most thought they would have to sit writing all day, because they thought many dogs bark so much and so often. But after keeping records for a whole week, they often document that the dog in question had barked only two to five minutes a day, in some cases only twenty seconds, in other cases not at all for an entire day or two.

Using a record-keeping chart for a week, being as precise as possible, will give you a much more realistic picture of how much the dog actually does bark, instead of how much you thought he barked. You will also have a clearer picture of the reasons why the dog was barking.

You can do this for many other behaviors as well. It is a good way of getting more reliable information. We humans often have a tendency of thinking and believing we know what is happening, but our perception, in reality, is often wrong or misleading. Hence the value of record-keeping.

Here is an example of the barking record-keeping chart my students use:

Barking Record Keeping Chart Examples

Date	Barking Starts	Barking Stops	How Long?	How does the barking sound?	Where is the dog?	What is he barking at?	What is he doing? (movements, etc.)

Date	Barking Starts	Barking Stops	How Long?	How does the barking sound?	Where is the dog?	What is he barking at?	What is he doing? (movements, etc.)
6/10	09:03	09:03	12 sec.	sounds angry	at window	a cat	jumping up and down
6/10	17:10	17:13	3 min.	hysterical	at window	kids running	stopped because I took him away
7/10	19:28	19:29	1 min. 5 sec.	angry	at door	guests arriving	standing at door, sniffing, jumping stopped when guests came in

You may be surprised by what your record-keeping results show about your dog's barking behavior.

Barking Classifications

Barking is often divided into five major classifications; however I have added a sixth because I think it is a little special. This is the most precise classification I can provide at this point in time, but I suspect that when more attention is given to this topic by researchers, we might get even more groupings. I have already received some indications from current studies being conducted that the list below might be added to.

The different barking types generally recognized now are:

1. Excitement barking

2. Warning barking

3. Fear barking

4. Guard barking

5. Frustration barking

6. Learned barking

Each of them will be reviewed in the following chapters.

3   Excitement Barking

Excitement barking expresses emotions ranging from happiness to the excited expectation of something good about to happen. This is a generally pleasurable kind of barking to experience, and my hope is that everybody has a dog who engages in this kind of barking. It occurs when the dog is happy or expecting something good is going to happen. It can reflect a certain level of stress as well, although this type of stress is not generally considered unhealthy with a few exceptions. Common examples include when owners or guests arrive at home, when the dog becomes aware he is on the way to the park or other place where some fun is awaiting, when you ask the dog to go out for a walk, and other situations where the dog gets excited. Excitement barking is easily recognized in terms of how it sounds and the movements of the dog associated with it.

How it sounds. It is a high frequency sound, and it can sound a little hysterical. Barking is more or less constant, or is a series of barks with small breaks in a sequence. Whining can occur in between the barking.

Activity involved. Because of his excitement level, the dog will probably exhibit a higher stress level than usual. Normally that means the dog will be moving because when his muscles are full of adrenalin, it is impossible for him to keep still. So the activity pattern will often include jumping up and down, spinning around, running here and there—and in some cases everything at one time! His tail will usually be wagging—most people know that a wagging tail means the dog is happy or excited. The dog can actually wag its tail for other reasons also, but almost always will when he is excited.

Most dogs get excited and will bark when you arrive home.

If you use an obedience command in a situation like this, like asking the dog for a down or sit, you will often get whining or yawning or other calming signals. The dog just cannot keep still because of the high excitement/stress level—just like people do when we are very excited about something. Interestingly enough, many dogs will want to have something in their mouths, so they pick up something and run around with it.

If the dog gets overly-excited but has no possibility of moving or taking something in his mouth (for instance when being held tight on a short leash), or if he has a chronically high stress levels due to other things going on in his life, you might see exaggerated reactions such as:

- jumping up

- hysterical barking

- biting on leash and trouser legs, even legs

- running round knocking things over

- pulling the leash violently

- lunging at other dogs, or cars, or other things

Should you reprimand this? Of course you should not punish a dog for being happy or excited. By listening to how the barking sounds and seeing what situation the dog is in, you should be able to determine if this is excitement barking. If it is, you should not reprimand or punish the dog for it, nor should you be angry with him. At least you should not show it. Don't punish joy!

What can we do about it? Right away you must choose what your response should be, and you do have a number of suitable choices:

1. Be calm yourself. Your calmness will influence the dog.

2. Have some objects available and let the dog carry one of them. If the dog picks up one himself, let him carry it. It is quite difficult to bark and carry something at the same time! Some might make some muffled noises, but it will not be so disturbing. And also having something in his mouth might have a calming effect. This will not teach the dog not to bark, but at least you stopped the barking temporarily. If the dog reacts to a knock on your door, having a technique to quiet the barking for at least some

Giving your dog a favorite toy to hold in his mouth can provide an alternative behavior to barking.

amount of time will make your guests a little more comfortable coming into your home.

3. Ask the dog to fetch something for you, then let him search and find it and bring it to you. The dog keeps himself active and does something useful at the same time, and you have been able to channel something irritating into something useful. Of course this means you have to first teach him to search for and retrieve objects before you can use it in the actual situation.

4. If the dog is only a little agitated, it can help to have the dog sit for just a few seconds before answering or going

out the door (or before a similar exciting activity). Three seconds is usually enough, but I would not overdo the sitting because of the stress level. Use a hand signal for the sit, without saying anything. If a dog is stressed and excited, he will be more apt to pick up a visual signal. Dogs are visual by nature, and his hearing is often blocked in a stressful situation. Besides that, if you are irritated by the barking, it may come out if you try to give a verbal command.

Have your dog sit for a second or two before opening the door: no words, just the hand signal for sit.

If the dog has started to engage in excitement barking before you can take measures to reduce it, make sure that he does not get any inadvertant reward for barking. Try holding your hand above the dog's nose for three to five seconds without saying anything. When you do reward the dog for his silence (either with a treat or letting him outside, for example), you want to make sure he does not associate the reward with barking, but rather with his silence. Otherwise they can easily learn:

1. bark

2. sit

3. be rewarded

Of course, that was not the intention! This learning by "backward chaining" can occur when you accidentally chain the wrong behavior to the right behavior as in this example.

Training Techniques

When You Come Home
If your dog becomes excited and barks noisily when you come home, try the following steps:

1. Open the door, walk in slowly, say hello quietly to your dog, and give him a little pat or other gentle physical contact, just enough so the dog knows you have acknowledged him.

2. Walk quietly further on into the house, take off your jacket, put away groceries, etc.

3. Let the dog have some time to calm down.

4. If you have been away a long time, and know that your dog likely needs to go outside, then just take him quietly and without any fuss outside to do his business.

5. Then go back in again, saving a longer walk for later.

By all means you should give him the kind of attention listed above when you come home. He has been waiting for you.

Do not make him feel frustrated and sad by ignoring him completely. Think about how you yourself would feel if it had been you. Dogs have the same feelings, and they need to feel that you care about them.

The key is making your arrival at home calm and pleasant. If you do the dog will be calmer also. Very often hysterical greetings on the part of the dog are a direct result of making too much fuss when we come home. Playing, fussing, and thereby winding them up makes matters worse.

If the reason for the excitement barking is that the dog has actually been left too long alone at home, and has become desperate about it, you probably need to think about other solutions, like a babysitter, a doggy daycare, or similar solution.

When Guests Arrive at the Door
A ringing doorbell or knock at the door provides a signal to the dog that guests are arriving. Most dogs get excited and start to bark—because they find guests fun and stimulating.

You must be careful in this case not to get angry, yell at the dog, jerk on the leash, or punish the dog in any other way. If you do that, the dog can then easily start associating people with unpleasant things, and ending up being afraid of them. This just creates a much worse problem. If we inadvertently teach the dog to be afraid of people, he will become defensive toward them and may begin to show aggressive behaviors.

If your dog gets overly excited and barks when guests arrive, try the following steps:

1. If the dog runs barking to the door, calmly follow him. Then move yourself into a position so that you are between the dog and the door, with your back to the dog.

2. Wait until the dog calms down a little. He will likely do this because by positioning yourself between him and the door you have shown him that that you are taking responsibility for the situation. He will know what it means.

3. Grasp the doorknob. Open the door a few inches at a time stopping every time the dog starts barking again. Stand still until the dog is quiet.

4. Then you can start talking to the guest through the opening, explaining that you are training the dog. Tell the guest whatever he needs to know about the dog.

5. Let your guest in. Have your guest either turn away from the dog until he is calmer, or you can gently take hold of your dog's collar and hold the dog a step away.

6. Go into the living room or wherever you want to sit. Sit down. No fussing, just be calm. It is usually amazing how quickly the dog calms down then.

Place yourself between the dog and the door and then wait for calm before opening the door.

If there are other people in the house when guests arrive, one can hold the dog calmly and gently while the other one is opening the door and greeting the guest. Do not give the dog any kind of attention if he is excited. Gently hold his collar without pulling—removing the possibility the dog may run up to the guest. Do not grab the dog's fur, and absolutely do not hold him by the neck.

Once everyone has sat down, the best thing to is to have the dog on a leash, so he can be together with you, looking at the guest, but not able to go over to him. When the dog has calmed down, which he will do amazingly fast if you just ignore him and do not command him or give him any other kind of attention, you can let go of the leash so he can interact with the guest if he wants to. The guest should be instructed not to start fussing or playing with the dog, just basically say hello. If the guest cannot comply with that, the best option is to keep the dog with you.

Have your guest calmly greet your dog.

In the Car

The reason for barking in the car is that, for most dogs, being taken for a drive in the car means that they are going some place where fun things happen: training, dog parks, and other venues where they expect some excitement.

One strategy to reduce barking in the car is to take your dog on many short trips. Have your dog sit and wait for you in the car while you go to post office, bank, shop, doctor, and so on. During this period of training, I recommend making many trips every day, each of them short and boring. Sometimes take the dog out for a little sniff, calmly, and then head back to the car again.

You might still get a little barking and whining near real fun places the dog has been before, but sometimes we must accept some excess barking in cases like this as a compromise.

Barking in a car in anticipation of going somewhere exciting.

Here's an example of the strategy mentioned above. A hunting dog barked hysterically every time he got into the car. His owners could not take him to shops or to visit people because the noise drove them crazy and caused their baby to scream. It turned out that the dog had rarely been in the car except for when they were going to go hunting in the forest—which, of course, was what he loved best. His expectations were very high, and it created a high level of stress every time he was taken to the car.

The training I put up for them was quite simple. For a month, the owner was asked to take the dog for small, boring car trips as many times a day as he could manage. Then only take the dog out of the car now and then for a little sniff around places like gas stations, parking lots, and so on.

I didn't hear from the owner for awhile, so I was curious about how the training turned out. A few months later one of their neighbors called wanting a private lesson. When he came I just had to ask about the barking hunting dog who lived nearby. It turns out that was why he had come to me. He had been so impressed at how quickly the dog had learned to keep still in the car. The dog really had learned to keep quiet—he barked only a little when the car turned into the last little dirt road that took them to the hunting grounds. But the owner accepted that happily, understanding the excitement he himself felt at the thought of the hunt.

At the Sight of Other Dogs

This kind of barking is very often misunderstood. Some owners think they have an aggressive dog and try to punish him for it. They don't know that barking is not the same as aggression. On the contrary, a barking dog is usually not aggressive. In fact, some people have known this for as long as humans have had dogs. There is a saying from Viking times a thousand years ago: "Barking dogs never bite." Well, they probably do, but usually only if cornered and threatened. Any dog will bite then.

Other dogs are very interesting to most dogs. It usually starts very early in a dog's life. A young dog will be excited when he sees another dog, and will often start barking. If the barking becomes hysterical, the reason can be one of two:

1. It can be that the dog has always played either too much or too wildly with other dogs. This causes stress levels to go up at the sight another dog, and the excitement and stress makes him bark.

2. The other reason may be that he rarely meets other dogs and gets hysterical when he does see one.

Puppies and young dogs need to be in the presence of other dogs to develop their social skills, but it should not be through playing only. When play becomes too exciting at this age, puppies will not learn the fine points about being social. They need different forms of social contact rather than frantic play. Now and then, a little playing with other puppies of approximately the same size and age is acceptable. Their play should not last too long, usually not more than ten minutes, sometimes shorter. It should be stopped before they become so excited and stressed that they overdo things.

Puppies need play time, but limit it so they do not become stressed.

While calm play is beneficial, as soon as a puppy can take walks, the best thing to do is to find other dogs to take walks with. Perhaps on a leash in the beginning, but later off leash when it is appropriate. To go for walks together means being together, but also having other things to be interested in—smells, sights, sounds, and new things they can focus their curiosity on. Puppies learn about the world by using all their senses. Walking together also means they do not become so hectic and intense with each other, and the relationship between them becomes more relaxed and natural.

Have your puppy meet nice adult dogs—they need to have role models. If they only play with other puppies, they will think that is how it is always going to be (chasing, wrestling, nipping, etc.). They do not learn the finer social skills such as to have some self control or how to behave as an adult. You should also sit with your dog looking at other dogs at a distance, from both inside your house or while outside.

Standing with your dog at a distance watching other dogs is a good strategy.

In other words, a puppy needs several types of social contact with other dogs if he is going to grow up as a well-functioning, social adult. Then you will not get the hysterical barking at other dogs that becomes such a problem for both people and dogs.

If you have an adult dog who still exhibits hysterical behavior in the presence of other dogs, you need to start the process of teaching the dog to be social as you would with a puppy. Walks with other dogs are still the best thing you can do in this case. I call it parallel walking, where you walk in the same direction with other owners and dogs to take away the threat and stress that meeting other dogs involves. Provide plenty of distance between the dogs and walk in the same direction in a relaxed fashion. This has proven to be the most effective method I have ever used to remove the stress in dog to dog interactions. I use it a lot.

Excitement Barking Due to Chronic Stress

Barking due to chronic stress needs to be dealt with differently than the kinds of excitement barking mentioned above. Unlike the simple and practical things that apply elsewhere, barking caused by chronic stress means you will need to address the underlying factors otherwise you will never get to the bottom of the problem.

Keep in mind if your dog is overreacting to things, he likely has a high level of stress. And if he does, it won't matter how much you work and train him—rather you need to find out what is stressing the dog, and do something about that.

Chronic stress can arise inadvertently if the dog's owners engage in the following activities or behaviors to excess:

- Throwing balls and sticks and Frisbees™.

- Kicking balls and stones.

- Bicycling, jogging and other kinds of repetitive activity.

- Playing every day with other dogs or owners.

- Owners who are frequently angry or aggressive.

- High demands placed on the dog given his experience, ability to concentrate, and mental development.

While some exercise is beneficial, if you provide your dog too much physical activity it can lead to high stress levels.

Chronic stress can arise from the environment or the way the dog is raised including:

- Too little rest and sleep.

- Too little food and water—especially for puppies.

- Lack of close contact with owners and other dogs.

- Too much time spent alone.

- Not being given the opportunity to relieve himself when he needs to.

- Too much noise and people running around in the house.

- Too little freedom of movement, especially when a lot of time is spent in crates, kennels, or being tied up.

- Too many threatening things such as strangers, frequent storms, etc.

Whatever the reasons for stress, we know now that stress over time makes us sick. Occasional stress once in a while is okay, as the body will recover. Every day over time is not okay. Every time your dog gets stressed, hundreds of biochemical processes start in his body. At least one hormone (Neuropetide Y) attacks the immune system. If stressful things happen too often, the body will get a chronically high stress level, and the immune system will be impacted. The dog will get sick. All kinds of infections, indeed almost every kind of illness can be traced back to stress.

Don't Reward the Wrong Behavior

Be careful of what you are rewarding when dealing with unwanted excitement barking. Any kind of attention given at the wrong time can be viewed as a reward by the dog. Such attention can include:

- talking to the dog

- looking at the dog

- touching the dog

This also means that distractions can be a reward, commands can be a reward, even punishment and yelling can also be rewards. If you yell at the dog at the moment he barks, he might stop then and there, but only because he is startled. Once he finds out what happened, he will most probably bark again later, because of the attention he received. In other words, he didn't learn anything.

What to Stay Away From

There are some things you must try to avoid if the dog is barking excessively due to excitement:

- Do not yell at or punish a happy dog who is barking.

- Do not pull or jerk on the leash, do not pinch ears.

- Do not use citronella collars, shock collars, or squirt water at the dog.

- Giving attention to the barking that can be rewarding to the dog.

- Expecting calm behavior in a stressed dog because of the high level of stress hormones in the muscles. You must address the underlying causes of stress.

- Ignoring a dog full of happy expectations. Do not sit down and read the paper every time the dog gets excited at the thought of going outside. Think about when a child is going to a party. What if every time the child shows joy, you sit down and you wait. Can you imagine the tears, frustrations and unhappiness this would cause? I do not believe you would even think about doing this to a child. So why do it to your dog?

- Displaying yo-yo emotions with a dog (happy then distraught, happy then frustrated) as this can extinguish happiness in the dog. This will cause the dog to become frustrated and sad and also depressed. Yes, he might give up and be calmer. But he will feel terrible, and many dogs get depressed for this reason.

Don't always spoil a dog's excitement. Let him express his joy from time to time.

Summing up Excitement Barking

Excitement barking can be heard as a high pitched series of barks.

The situation will tell you if the dog is excited, and for what reason.

The activity will involve lot of movement on the part of the dog. You must try to diffuse his energy through alternative behaviors (holding something in his mouth) or acting calmly yourself.

What you do about it depends completely on the situation, the personality of your dog, and what the dog gets excited about.

Do not inadvertently reward or reinforce the barking.

Remember that some excitement barking should be permitted so the dog can express himself.

4 The Warning Bark

The warning bark is a vocal expression you will not hear as often as other types of barking. But you will hear some dogs use it in situations where they perceive others in the pack (dog or human) need some sort of warning.

How it sounds. One short, sharp "woof," meaning simply: "Get away, the enemy is coming."

Activity involved. Flight from the threat is common. In pack animals, in some cases, one of the pack will stay back and take the "responsibility" to defend the rest.

The warning bark was probably the first type of bark that people recognized—and found useful. Our ancestors needed to be very aware of their natural surroundings and presence of nearby wild animals. They were able to take advantage of the warning barks that wild dogs—who often were attracted to human camp sites to search for food scraps—would give each other. (I have no doubt that dogs were just as good at finding food then as they are now!) They would sneak around the bonfire waiting for leftovers—and then warn the others when enemies or predators were approaching. That helped people defend themselves. Of course nobody can prove this was the case, but I find it very believable.

Recently I had the pleasure of helping to watch over a litter of seven Leonberger puppies. At six weeks of age, they were allowed to go in and out of the house as they wanted. So they were often out in the garden where they had lots of fun in an enriched environment. One day a stranger approached them without me being around, and the mother of the puppies spotted the stranger and gave one sharp bark. Immediately all of the puppies ran directly into the house. No question about it—they knew exactly what the bark meant. The mother stayed out to keep an eye on things. Eventually things went back to normal.

In many cases I have seen dogs give this warning bark to their human families. Often the people do not understand it, so they do not react in any way, or maybe even tell the dog to be quiet. The dogs then get stressed and frustrated, and might start to bark more, trying to make the people "listen." After having experienced this over time, the dog will learn that it doesn't help to give a single warning bark, so he might start to bark in a more constant fashion when facing a perceived threat. All of a sudden you have a barking problem.

A typical warning bark situation.

What can we do about it? Since a dog might think his job is to warn the pack about danger and since this is a natural thing to for a dog to do, we humans should react in some way to show we understand what the dog is expressing. Of course, you cannot run away and hide like the puppies did. But it is important to communicate to the dog that you have got the message, and that you will now take over responsibility for dealing with the threat. Just like another dog or a wolf might do.

The simplest thing to do is to calmly place yourself between the dog and what appears to be the threat. This could be a person, an animal, a machine, or the sound of something unseen. Dogs do this, horses do this. They split up—or go in between—the threat and the other animal. This is one of the simplest and most efficient techniques to use to inform the dog you heard him and are in charge. It works because dogs understand it and they do it themselves.

The scenario will look something like this:

- A sound or something is heard or seen. The dog barks to warn.

- Get up calmly up without looking at or talking to the dog.

- Place yourself in front of the dog, between him and the sight or sound, with your back to the dog (this is non-threatening). Hold your hands a little out from your body (not stretching them towards the dog!) with the palms of your hands visible.

- Stand still. Wait till the dog is quiet or turns around and goes the other way, which he will do after awhile, because you are so clearly signaling "I am going to take care of this."

Later on when the dog has become a little more experienced, you do not need to move, you can use the hand signal alone.

Splitting up in action. The owner is using a hand signal and placing himself between the "threat" and the dog to reassure him there is nothing to fear.

Warning Bark Cases

🐾 I live in the forest way out in the countryside where there are wild animals around me all the time. One winter a moose was causing problems, getting into the garden every night, eating the branches off the fruit trees. The dogs warned me every time he got close—several times each night. I got very tired of being woken up all the time. I decided to put a stop to it, so for a couple of nights I got up every time the dogs warned about the moose and got in front of them to show I was going to deal with the moose myself.

The third night they stopped warning me. They had reached the point where they knew I would take responsibility. I slept the whole night after that, but of course every one of my apple trees was eaten! The technique was effective, but maybe not the smartest thing to do in that case!

🐾 When people approached the farm, my dog Saga usually ran to the gate and "welcomed" them, giving me a warning bark that they were there. I would go to the gate, place myself in front of her and say hello to the person before letting him in.

Whenever I was away, no one else could be bothered to do it, and so that left the job to Saga. She started to be very intense in her barking. When I returned from a trip, I had to do the job of training her all over again. Then we were back to normal.

Frankly I enjoy having my dogs warn me about strangers because I live so far out into the woods—and so they always do it.

🐾 A colleague of mine had adopted a sweet and friendly dog with one little problem: at night she barked at everything that moved, from leaves falling to cars passing by. The colleague knew very well the basic principles of taking over the responsibility for protection from the dog, and had placed the dog on the other side of her bed, so she was closest to the window herself. It did not help.

My colleague just couldn't force herself to get up at night. She was very tired and just couldn't do it. So she asked me if I had any ideas of other things to do. I asked if she could try a compromise—such as just lifting herself up a little on one elbow, and stretching out one arm/hand toward the dog. She said she would try, and it worked. After two nights, the dog stopped barking, and the problem was solved.

Sometimes it takes very little in the way of visual signals before the dog gets the point. Dogs are visual by nature, and they pick up much quicker on things they see than things they hear—like being talked to.

Summing Up the Warning Bark

The warning bark is meant to warn the pack about possible danger.

It is a short, sharp "woof."

Respond to it by showing the dog that you have heard the warning and you are taking over the responsibility to act against the threat.

5 Fear Barking

Almost all dogs are, of course, afraid of certain things—anything else would be unnatural. Fear levels range from just slightly worried to a full panic. When an individual feels fear, his stress level goes up, and this is normal because the stress system is part of a dog's survival skills. For example, if a dog is not in a position to cope with fear, and he cannot run away for some reason, strong emotions will often come out through the mouth instead. In other words, the dog will bark.

We humans also make sounds when we are afraid, especially when we are not able to escape or get away from what we fear. Dogs are not different from us that way.

How it sounds. This bark will be high pitched, and come in long series of barks. It is similar to excitement barking, but you will very clearly hear the fear in the dog's voice. This long series of hysterical barking will sometimes end in a howl, a call for help, like when a puppy calls for his mother to come.

Activity involved. Because of the high stress level involved, the dog will be active, his muscles full of adrenalin. The movements will be different from excitement barking. The dog will be restless, running back and forth, looking out windows, scratching on doors, trying to get out. Sometimes they will start chewing on objects, or sometimes on themselves. In a few cases they become completely apathetic.

Should you reprimand this? Of course you cannot punish the dog for being afraid! If you do the dog will only become more afraid. Unfortunately it is a fact that fear barking is the kind of barking people punish most often and most severely. Maybe it is because the sound is so penetrating and heartbreaking. But whatever your feelings are, do not punish your dog! That is why you need to gain knowledge about fear barking so it can be handled a different way.

Levels of Fear

There are several levels of fear we see in dogs that are expressed in barking:

- **A little uncertain**. This is quite normal and natural. The dog is wary or skeptical about something and he usually will be able to handle it if you do not interfere. It is curiosity that usually makes them investigate whatever is bothering them. They may choose just to move away from the source of their anxiety; it is their choice, and quite OK.

- **Worried**. In this case the dog will usually not dare to investigate. Do not fuss about this, or push/pull the dog in any way. Just wait and see what happens, or walk over and interact with what is bothering the dog yourself. I have patted many mail boxes and statues in my time! But do not say anything and do not try to make the dog approach. His curiosity usually takes over when he sees you going up to the feared object confidently.

- **Startled**. The dog's typical reaction is to jump in response to a loud noise. This is a natural response; people do it all the time and are not called nervous wrecks because they startle like this. Stay calm, pay no attention to it. If the dog wants to investigate, let him do it.

- **Fearful**. The dog will respond to fear by beginning to exhibit calming signals. If the calming signals are not successful, the dog will likely begin to show symptoms of stress, go into defensive mode, often growling, and then will try to get away. The dog should be removed from this situation, or be provided some other help.

- **Really afraid**. No calming signals will appear. The dog will immediately want to defend himself and likely will growl and snap. Then he will likely try to get away, or failing that, will try to deal with the cause of his fear by lunging and maybe biting. You need to get the dog out of this situation!

- **Panic**. The dog cannot think or function anymore. The dog is likely to bite whatever or whoever is closest to him, even his owner if he is holding him. Yelling at the dog, or using punishment will, of course, only make it worse. The dog is not coping. In some cases the dog will become completely apathetic and will not appear to hear or see or react to anything. In this case you must once again get the dog out of the situation. Do not stay there and hope it will pass. It will not. The dog can go into shock, and that is dangerous and life threatening.

What Do Dogs Fear?

Dogs can become afraid of practically anything; it depends on the situation and circumstances, as well as the dog's experiences and mental state. Just like with people.

Some of the most common things dogs fear include:

- Being left alone at home, in a car, in a kennel, or tied up.

- Sudden and/or loud sounds.

- Threatening behavior of people and other dogs.

- Anger ("aggression") in the dog's home environment and/ or from pack members.

- Being held tight, losing freedom of movement.

- Exposure to new or strange objects.

- And many other things depending on experiences, history, mental state, and learned ability to cope.

One thing is absolutely certain: we cannot know for sure what a dog is going to be (or not be) afraid of. If a dog is afraid, he is afraid—and that is that! We just have to work on it from there.

Fear is not something a dog is necessarily born with. A dog can be more prone to becoming easily afraid, but he need not necessarily ever be an easily frightened individual. That is up to us. Fear

Dogs may react fearfully to a wide variety of objects and begin to bark in response to a perceived threat. You can touch the object to show it is OK, but do not look at the dog or bend towards him as this lady does.

is learned through experiences and associations. And because it is learned, it can also be un-learned. In theory, a dog can overcome his fears. In reality, it can be difficult sometimes depending on the circumstances the dog is living under, the dog's age, health and probably a number of other things as well.

How Does a Dog Develop Fear?

Many scientists have done studies and research on fear in people over the years, so there is a lot of documentation on how fear is learned and how it can be overcome. A classic research study concerns a little boy name Albert and a mouse. It pops up in almost every psychology book.

The researchers put Albert in a room with a white mouse. He sat there petting the mouse without being afraid at all. While he was petting the mouse, the researchers scared the boy by making some terrible noise. He associated the frightening noises with the mouse, and so over time became afraid of the mouse.

You can never tell beforehand exactly what kind of associations will be made relating to fear. It is the same with dogs. If you jerk

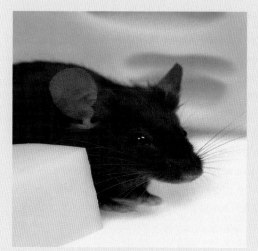

Even something as harmless as a mouse can be a source of fear if the presence of the mouse is associated with something frightening.

49

on the leash to stop a dog from pulling, he might associate the pain with anything he was focused on at the time. In that way he can become afraid of dogs, cars, kids, or whatever. He will probably not associate it with pulling on a leash.

A Step-by-Step Method for Dealing with Fear

Researchers have also worked on how people and animals learn not to fear, and found that the only way to do it is by what is termed systematic desensitization and counter-conditioning. That sounds complicated and rather heavy, so we usually call it the step-by-step method. That is the method you can use to change a dog's fear. So let us look at it.

The goal is to help the dog to not be afraid of whatever was causing him fear. Begin your training at a distance from whatever the dog fears and in a situation where the dog feels comfortable. Depending on what the dog is afraid of, your course of action can vary. However, the overall plan is that you move step-by-step closer toward what the dog fears (a person, another dog), all the time being careful that you do not go too quickly and make the dog feel uncomfortable.

To take the example of little Albert mentioned above, the process to help him overcome his fear of the mouse could have looked like this. Albert is placed in one end of the room, perhaps eating something he really likes, or doing something enjoyable. The mouse would be exposed for a short moment in the other end of the room. It is repeated a little later. If Albert is fine with this, the mouse can be exposed for a second longer, and then for gradually longer and longer periods of time. Then you can start moving closer step by step, being sure all the time that Albert is feeling good about it. The goal is reached when Albert can once again sit petting the mouse and enjoy it.

Fear of Being Home Alone

Teaching a puppy to not fear being alone at home is one of the most important things you can do as an owner. It is usually quite easy if you let the puppy feel at home first. If he feels safe and looks upon it as his home, and he isn't forced to be alone very long or very suddenly in the beginning, most puppies have no difficulties learning to be alone at home. Leaving the puppy alone must be done little by little, so the puppy's first weeks in his new home must be carefully planned.

If the dog has already learned to be afraid of being alone, it will take a little longer to make him feel safe again, but it is definitely possible. Depending on how afraid he is, you can plan the step-by-step training in different ways. As with all problems like this, you must remove the cause of the fear. In this case, the dog must not be left alone in the beginning. You have to find a solution, ranging from family members taking a holiday to be with the dog, or finding a dog-sitter, or maybe it is possible for you to bring your dog to work. A good doggy daycare can also be a solution, but not all daycares are good ones.

Once the dog is less stressed about being left alone, you can begin to apply some training to the problem. You should begin by teaching the dog a visual hand signal—the palm of the hand held up toward the dog. First, use this hand signal while in a seated position. Then get up and sit right back down again. When the dog seems to understand that the hand signal is an indication that you will indeed return, you can proceed to use it when you go into other rooms in the house. Give your hand signal, walk through a door, and then come right back. Then do the same thing but, close the door behind you, wait a few seconds, and then and come right back. Begin to lengthen the time you are "gone," going from a few seconds to a few minutes. But always give the hand signal before you leave. The dog will learn then that you will come back.

Teach the dog a visual hand signal.

Teaching your dog to accept being alone in the house is a much better solution than putting a dog in an outside kennel run or tied up outside for a period of time. You cannot be 100% sure someone or something won't bother the dog. Dogs can be stolen, or teased, or scared in many ways. If the dog has a bad experience because of scary things happening while outside (such as firecrackers or kids throwing things at the dog), then you have to insure that this doesn't happen again, and definitely not while you are trying to teach the dog to be alone at home, you will never make it. Overall, I would think at least twice before leaving a dog alone outside to cure him of his fear of being left alone in your home.

Leaving a dog tied up outdoors runs the risk of having the dog become fearful of a variety of other things that he would not encounter if left inside your home.

What to Do About Fear Barking

There are a number of steps you can take to prevent or treat fear barking:

1. Avoid whatever is making the dog afraid enough to start barking, especially during the time that you are training him to stop fear barking. Sometimes you can avoid the dog becoming scared if you just think a little, by not putting him in a threatening position, and by teaching him to cope with things a little at a time.

2. If the dog has bad reactions to sounds or other things when you are together with him, be careful not to show any reaction yourself. Do not talk to him, soothe him, or pet him. Just act as though nothing had happened, and the dog will be more likely to forget about it.

3. Do not pull or force or coax the dog into a situation where he doesn't feel safe. Wait, keep a loose leash, and let the dog decide if he can manage the situation or not. If he does not, turn around, and move away from what is threatening before starting over. Done properly, the dog will usually be able to proceed because he was given a choice. Then curiosity takes over, which normally results in the dog deciding what was bothering him was not so scary after all.

4. Go between the dog and the scary thing, acting as a barrier. Dogs do this splitting behavior themselves, and therefore they will understand that you are taking responsibility, and that they do not have to worry. This is a brilliant technique that can be used in many cases.

5. Avoid an oncoming threatening situation by curving away from it or changing directions. This increases the space between the dog and the threat. Sometimes I see a dog trying to get on the other side of his owner, thereby

having the owner act as a barrier. Let him do that! Dogs will curve if they have the chance, so do not stop them by forcing them back into heeling position. Life is not an obedience exercise. A dog will naturally create distance and change direction to avoid a conflict.

To act as a barrier, go between a dog and what he is reacting to, looking away from the dog, not turning toward him. Do not bend at all in the direction of your dog.

6. Teach the dog to cope with a threatening situation gradually. Flooding—exposing a dog to a threat with no warning usually at close proximity—will only create stressed and fearful dogs. Let your dog learn to cope with other dogs and people, sounds, smells, sights, at his own pace, and in his own way. Using his senses to investigate the world is the best way to let a dog learn to cope with all life's calamities. No commanding, no obedience—just let him see, smell, taste, and listen to everything around him. Your only job is to ensure that he is safe and to maintain a loose leash. This is what I call "vaccinating" the

dog against being fearful or angry when he grows up. So far it is the most efficient method I have seen used to teach dogs to cope with almost anything that turns up. The dogs I have had the chance to use this "vaccination" program with all learned to cope with life as long as they lived.

7. Counter-conditioning can be a very effective method, using praise, food or other rewards in the presence of something threatening. Just watch out for backward chaining so the dog does not believe he is being rewarded for barking.

Methods That Will Not Work With Fear Barking

If a dog barks because he is afraid, it will not help to put the dog in a crate or into a small closed room. He will probably become even more afraid if you do so and react to this action as a punishment. This will result in some really negative and unnecessary associations. In other words, the problem will just get worse.

It will not help to squirt water or use citronella collars, shock collars, or anything else that causes the dog to be uncomfortable. Even if the barking stops right there and then, the lasting effects of using these methods will be worse. You end up inadvertently teaching him behaviors that are much worse for you, the environment, and the dog itself. That is how many dogs become so called "aggressive" because the fear has escalated to a dangerous level. It is so unnecessary.

Fear Barking Cases

🐾 I was out walking my dog with another owner and her Bearded Collie. The two dogs were playing together while they walked. I was not well acquainted with the neighborhood, and the other owner suddenly said she hoped there would be no shooting that day because her dog was terrified of gunfire. As soon as she said it, there was a shot, and then three things happened at the same time: (1) the dog startled and looked up—at the owner; (2) the owner turned quickly to the dog and was going to speak to him; and (3) I grabbed the lady's arm, turned her away from the dog and demanded that she not say anything. When I looked back, the two dogs were playing together again.

Was this dog fearful? No, but she might have become so because the owner started to make a fuss about the shooting and the result would have been fear barking. Be sure not to do that! Many dogs actually learn to be afraid that way. It is natural to be startled—I startled just as much as the dog did! But for both of us it was just because of the surprise, it had nothing to do with being afraid.

Some dogs startle more quickly and obviously than others—that does not mean a certain breed or individual is more nervous. The quick responses some dogs have to sudden movements and sounds have to do with the work they were bred to do. Herding dogs are typical of this.

🐾 A little dog was afraid of being groomed and became real panicky easily. If the groomer and owner tried to hold him, he barked, snapped, and then bit, and if they tied him up tightly so he couldn't bite, he stood shivering and salivating. It was really terrible to see. The reason for his fear was that he had been forced to stand for hours during grooming. You can imagine how that is for a little dog. Then his skin got sore and began giving him real pain—it must have been like torture.

In this case, the people involved had to learn to groom him in an understanding and nice way. Instead of hours, they need to do a little at a time, making the whole procedure more pleasant. Starting step by step, get the dog used to a brush again, no tie downs, no holding his hair in a painful way. Very, very short sessions, maybe only seconds in the beginning.

Often you have to do things differently from what you used to do. My best advice is: put yourself in the dog's place, try to feel how it is to be that dog now—maybe that is all you need to do things differently.

🐾 A little puppy was brought home by a proud mom. Dad was in the kitchen waiting for them. Mom opened the door, and the puppy saw the man inside. Unfortunately at the same time a broom stick fell down and hit the puppy.

Just an accident, but the shock terrified the puppy and a year and a half later, when they came to me for help, the dog was still terrified of the man and engaged in fear barking.

The dog was focused on the man when the broom stick hit her, and she therefore associated the unpleasantness with the man. That was how she became afraid, and that is how most dogs learn to be afraid of and bark at kids, other dogs, people, cars, and whatever. In so many cases we completely miss how dogs associate events.

🐾 I recently witnessed how a four month old puppy on her first walk in the village learned to be afraid of people in just seven seconds. A person came walking toward her, and the puppy, in puppy fashion, jumped happily toward the person. The owner pulled the puppy back—saying "No!" in a loud voice. The puppy looked a little bewildered. When another person approached, the puppy tried again to jump up and greet the person, a little more reluctantly this time. Same thing happened. The dog was pulled back harshly accompanied by a stern "No!" when a third person approached, this time the puppy hid behind her owner, tail between her legs.

This is essentially how dogs are often taught to be fearful of other dogs and people, especially kids. The owner thought she was saying essentially don't jump up on people. The dog learned that people were something to be afraid of and would likely become a fear barker over time.

Summing Up Fear Barking

When dogs are afraid of something, they will often start barking. The barking often sounds quite hysterical—you can hear the fear in the dog's voice.

If a dog is afraid, you must do something to help the dog. Do not make things worse by behaving in a way that will make the dog even more afraid.

Try to remove the possibility that the dog will become afraid.

Start training techniques such as where you use hand signals to assure the dog you will return and placing yourself as a barrier between the dog and whatever he finds threatening to reduce his fear.

Teaching a dog not to be afraid might take time, as it has to do with emotions. It may be the most time consuming training we have to do, but it is safe and sure. The best results are achieved if you do it carefully, step by step.

Understand and accept that it is natural for a dog to be afraid! He cannot help it, he is not afraid on purpose, and you must help him overcome it.

6   Guard Barking

This kind of barking is probably the most misunderstood of all. Because it usually is accompanied by growling sounds, people view it as the dog being aggressive, dominant, wanting to "take over," or other things that have nothing to do with it.

In the first place, aggression is really defensive and is based upon fear. A dog can be angry, of course, since a dog has many of the emotions we have. If we can accept that we sometimes are angry, we must also accept that dogs can be angry—especially if there is something to be angry about. Anger and defensive behavior is not a chronic state of mind. It almost always has to do with a specific situation.

So-called "aggression" can be expressed in different ways, but almost never in barking. If a dog needs to focus on defending himself or guarding, he cannot throw away a lot of energy into barking. The same applies to dominance—it has nothing to do with barking.

A barking dog guarding something has a high stress level at that moment in time. A so-called dominant dog will have all the self esteem in the world and probably feels in full control of himself and the situation. He will not be stressed enough to bark. "Dominant" dogs and dominant people are in control. It is only stressed and fearful individuals who yell and scream—and bark.

Guard barking occurs when a dog feels he is in a position where he has to defend himself or something that is his. The fear of losing something can be just as real as fearing for his own safety. He becomes unsure, stressed, and afraid. We do not become defensive if we have nothing to defend ourselves against.

How it sounds. If the dog is guard/defensive barking, there will usually be some growling in it. Something like:

Grrrrrr—bark, bark—grrrrr

The guard barking sound will generally be shorter and deeper than fear barking. But sometimes, when the dog is really afraid, it can sound more high pitched and similar to fear barking.

Activity involved. The dog will move forward, lunging towards the object he is defending himself against, trying to make it go away. When a dog goes into a defensive mode he might try to get away and out of trouble, or he might try to scare something or someone away by:

- showing teeth

- growling

- lunging forward

- snapping

- barking

- and eventually biting, but the bite comes at the very end, if nothing else helps

Should you reprimand this? Of course you should not reprimand the dog. If he feels he has to defend himself, you should assume he is completely convinced that he needs to do so. A reprimand here will make him become even more afraid than he already was. The more you punish the dog for going into defense mode, the more he will have a reason for doing it. He will become defensive and begin guard barking even more quickly in similar situations. For the dog, this behavior is part of his survival skills.

When your dog gets too close to another dog, he might react by lunging and barking to put more distance between himself and the other dog, especially if you haven't given him enough room during your approach.

What to Do About Guard Barking

It depends entirely on what the circumstances are that result in guard barking and what the dog is guarding or defending:

1. Avoid letting the dog get into a situation where he feels he has to defend himself. Maybe you have to change your own behavior, or protect the dog from encountering other people or dogs he may react badly to. This is a responsibility you have to take, as the dog's owner and family.

2. Be quicker to pick up the signals that the dog gives off as he begins to feel defensive. The dog will always give off a lot of calming or stress signals if you cannot avoid confrontations. Those signals will let you know that the dog is starting to feel threatened, unsure, and building up his defense. You need to learn to recognize these signals before they escalate into stronger emotions, such as the

Avoid putting a dog into a situation where he may be faced with having to defend himself.

dog starting to show teeth, growl, lunging, and so on. If the dog bites, we can only blame ourselves.

3. Early in a situation, before the dog finds it necessary to get defensive, you can show you are taking responsibility for things by going in between the dog and the object he reacts to (splitting).

4. Walk the dog in a curving pattern past approaching people or dogs since being approached directly and straight on is a threat for dogs. On his own, a dog will always politely adopt a curving approach as he passes by other dogs and people. Even just a slight change of direction is often enough.

Training Techniques

If a dog has learned to go quickly into a defensive mode, you might need to develop a training program to help the dog to cope. Many of these techniques are easy to implement and quite simple.

Parallel walking. If the dog has a problem with other dogs, people, kids, or specific kinds of people, like men with hats, I almost always start with an exercise called parallel walking. This means setting up a situation in which you walk with your dog on a leash, on a line apart, but parallel to whatever he fears. For example, if he has problems with other dogs, you and a friend should each walk beside each other with your dog on a leash, but with enough distance between the two of you to ensure the dog does not engage in a guard barking response. The distance can vary from dog to dog. Sometimes only three meters apart, in other cases 20 or 50 meters. In the worst cases I have worked with we had to start 300 meters apart. Some more tips include:

- It can help to have a barrier between the dogs. People can serve as that barrier, as can a fence or shrubs. But if there is no obvious barrier, you can do it by increasing the distance between the dogs.

- Walk slowly and in a relaxed fashion so the dog has time to relax and think about what is happening and has the chance to glance in the direction of the other dog.

- Ten to fifteen minutes of this is usually enough. The dogs tend to become very tired as a result of this training because they start thinking, and thinking can be exhausting.

Walk in a parallel fashion, maintaining as much distance between your dog and what he reacts to as needed to avoid a barking response, in this case a tall man. Over time, start to reduce the distance.

Walking in a curve. Make the dog follow you in a curve past approaching dogs or people. The size of the curve depends on the dog's reactions. Start with sufficiently wide curves, then quickly make them less and less wide. In the end, the curve can be almost symbolic.

Counter-conditioning. This is also called a "change of association." Place the dog well away from an object that he has had a negative reaction to in past—far enough so that he does not engage in guard barking. If he reacts to this situation calmly, you should praise and reward the dog. Providing the dog a positive association with something that he has reacted to negatively in the past will begin to change his attitude. When done correctly, the result can sometimes be almost magical. The trick is to be quick enough to grasp the right moment. If you are too slow (i.e., you reward after he starts to bark) it will likely have the opposite effect.

With all the above techniques, make sure that:

- The leash is not tight. Teach yourself to work with your dog on a loose leash.

- The dog has a soft and pleasant collar—a harness is even better.

- The dog is allowed to look at what he is worried about. Avoid doing anything that gets the dog to focus on you. He will not learn a thing about the other dog, for example, if he is looking at you all the time.

- Use no obedience commands. This is not the time to be obedient. The dog is learning to cope with things.

- Teach yourself and your dog a stopping hand signal—the palm of your hand towards your dog.

Use a hand stopping signal like this.

Try to avoid placing your dog in a position where he will be tempted to guard you or something else he values. Take away the possibility that the dog will want to start guarding if that is his tendency. If you put him in a position where he will want to engage in guarding, it will grow stronger and stronger every time you put him in that position. Do not tie your dog up outdoors, alone out in the garden, or left out on the balcony or an enclosed porch. Do not leave your dog alone in a crate, kennel or car where there is the slightest chance for people, dogs, or other things to bother him. Do not let the dog sleep in a place where people pass all the time, or guests come in.

Three Examples

One. Sara is hungry and waiting impatiently for her food. Once the food arrives, Sara begins to eat, but her owner has the idea that dogs should accept it when their food is taken away from them, so he takes the food away. Sara gets frustrated, but doesn't do anything the first time this happens. When he does it a second time, Sara growls to make him stop taking her food away—she is hungry. The owner continues to do this. Every time he takes the food away, Sara gets more and more frustrated because she cannot eat, and her defense of her food gets stronger and stronger. Later she will start growling the moment the food arrives, to try to tell the owner she really wants to have her food.

In a very short time she has learned to be food aggressive, which could so easily have been avoided. Food is necessary for survival, and a hungry dog will of course defend her food when it is taken away from her.

To avoid this happening, you should let dogs have their food to themselves, so they have nothing to defend. When the dog feels very sure he can have his food without being disturbed, he will not have any objection if it is taken away once in a while. A dog who trusts his owner will not go into a defensive mode. If you take that trust away, you will build up stronger and stronger defensive reactions including guard barking.

Think about yourself. You are very hungry and are given a plate full of lovely food. Then every time you stick a fork in it there is a person taking it away from you. How many seconds would it take before you got mad?

Two. I always let my dogs have their food without bothering them. I feel that is a right they have, just like with us. Because of that, they have complete trust in me. One day my German Shepherd was eating, and for some reason something fell down from a shelf and into his food just as he took a mouthful. I thought it looked like a sharp nail or something, so I just jumped at him, putting my hand into his mouth, down his throat, and got it out. He never blinked an eye, and just went on eating. If I had done this at every meal, he would soon have started to get very defensive—it does not take much imagination to figure that out.

One of the reasons people have for taking food away from their dogs is that they cannot be sure that a child might not come in and get into the dog's food bowl. But dogs usually eat their food in just a matter of seconds. If you are not capable of keeping kids away from the dog for that amount of time, I really question your position in the house. Close the kitchen door and let the dog eat without being disturbed. It cannot be that difficult.

Three. Prince is out walking with his owner when suddenly a jogger comes at him at high speed. Prince startles, starts to bark, and lunges forward to scare the jogger away. A normal reaction in this situation. The owner probably was also startled.

Things happening very suddenly will make a dog startle and cause his adrenalin to flow—and one of the results of this can be the dog barking. If an object suddenly comes straight toward a dog, he will usually view it as threatening. Remember, a sudden unexpected approach is very impolite in a dog's view of the world. If it happens more slowly, so they have time to do something about it, most dogs will start giving calming signals, like sniffing, curving, stopping, or looking away. If it happens very suddenly, they will immediately begin to try to scare whatever it is away.

When others are approaching, you start curving long before your dog has a chance to react, and you will be able to pass without a problem.

You can try very quickly to get your dog out into a curving position—not by pulling or dragging the dog—but by moving away yourself, or using a sound that to the dog means "follow me." See my book *My Dog Pulls. What Do I Do?* for more information on that cue. Or you can just stand still doing nothing. If the dog wants to move away from the situation, follow him.

Being angry or punishing the dog will only make the dog more stressed, and the association with joggers will become negative, so he learns to become angry with them. Teach yourself to get your dog out of situations like this in a nice way. Then you help your dog to cope, and the dog will not learn anything negative.

Summing Up Guard Barking

This kind of barking occurs when the dog feels compelled to guard or defend himself or something else. It means the dog feels threatened, and that he is trying to make whatever he is finding threatening to go away.

Guard barking often begins with growling sounds, then barking interspersed with more growls.

The dog will position his body in a forward manner, or move forward in lunges, attempting to scare the threat away. This is meant to keep the threat away, not to signal an immediate attack. The dog's focus will be on defense.

This kind of barking should not be punished. That will only encourage the dog to go into a defensive mode, and do it faster and stronger every time it happens. Such punishment becomes rather meaningless.

Planning, thinking ahead, and management are the keys to preventing guarding behaviors. Some breeds have stronger dispositions and tendencies to be defensive than others. If you have a dog with such genes, you must be aware of it, and be even more careful not to build up that dog's tendency to guard. It will be important to keep this in mind all the time, so you do not get more of this behavior than absolutely necessary.

What is also necessary is to understand that all dogs will defend themselves in a threatening situation, and that dogs, like all other species, have a right to defend their lives. That is one of the survival skills we all have. If they didn't have it in them, dogs would have become extinct long ago. The ability to defend their puppies, food, and last but absolutely not least themselves, is a survival mechanism we cannot ignore just because we do not like it.

A good rule is: Never be the one who makes a dog feel he has to defend himself.

7   Frustration Barking

This is a kind of barking that is heartbreaking to listen to. You can hear the desperation and frustration in the dog. If you hear this and follow the sound toward the dog, you will often find a dog that is tied up, is alone out of doors, is not being allowed to be with people, or is in a kennel. Loneliness is often the reason. Hunger can be another. Long term stress is always at the bottom of it.

How it sounds. The sound will be endless rows of static barking. The same tone over and over again, sometimes ending in a howl. Then the whole sequence is repeated.

Activity involved. Typically it is a behavior that is repeated over and over again in an endless fashion. Whether it is barking, digging, chewing, licking, chasing shadows or his tail—these behaviors, ironically, have a pleasant physical effect on the dog. It causes certain hormones to be released which make the dog feel a little better, and makes him better able to endure a terrible or hopeless situation.

We see the same in humans and other animals. In mental hospitals and in old people's homes, you will often see people repeating the same movements over and over again. They can rock back and forth, or repeat the same motions with fingers or hands. In stables, you see horses doing repetitive behaviors like weaving, chewing, sucking air, and other things. In wild life parks and zoos, it is common to see animals trot back and forth, back and forth, in a consistent path at the same speed and rhythm. These behaviors are performed by individuals in a terrible state of mind, and they do them to be able to survive while under a lot of stress.

Should you reprimand this? Punishment will, of course, not help. Punishment in these kinds of dull, boring, or stressful situations should be considered cruelty towards animals. The individual needs help, not punishment.

Dogs often will engage in frustration barking when a barrier prevents them from directly being able to interact with a person or another dog.

Frustration Barking Cases

I used to be a horse trainer long before I was a dog trainer, and I had a reputation for getting results with "difficult" horses. Long after I stopped training horses, I would get a horse now and then for rehabilitation from some desperate owner. It was always the same—the horse was at the end of his wits because of the treatment he had received.

One day I took in a purebred horse that had started to weave—rocking back and forth—in the stable. My solution was to let the horse go out and graze on grass, simply letting him have a real nice summer holiday. I continued this for several days, keeping him in the stable only at night, with plenty of hay to chew. The weaving behavior never showed up again. Eating is what horses do all the time, it is basically their lifestyle. When they get too little to chew, their legs automatically start wandering in a search of something to eat. In an enclosed area they will walk round and round, but if they are tied up, they start weaving. They need to be able to chew and move around freely, basic needs for horses. Everyone, people and dogs included, have basic needs that need to be accommodated.

A Beagle lived on a farm with an elderly couple. They had no experience with dogs and thought it best for the dog to be outside all the time. So they tied him up outside for hours at a time.

After a while the dog started to bark. When it became so chronic that they couldn't stand it, they would punish the dog severely. The stress the dog was suffering from did not go away, of course, and the dog felt even worse after the punishment. He started to dig instead, and dug holes everywhere. They didn't like that either, so they punished him for that as well. He had to find other outlets for his stress and frustration, so the next thing he did was to eat the wall of the house, and when they came to me he had chewed almost totally through the wall.

The solution was as simple as it was efficient:

1. Stop leaving the dog outdoors for long periods of time. I asked if they could have him indoors with them, and they had nothing against that. They just had thought he could not be indoors for some reason. So he was taken indoors and he curled happily up on the sofa.

2. In addition I suggested it would be nice if the owners could do something with the dog. Not much, and in this case the owners were not in good health, but the man used to walk down to the mailbox every day—1 km down the road. Could he take the dog with him, and let the dog sniff and explore as they walked? Yes, he could, and was happy to do it.

And that was all it took.

Dogs deserve to be allowed indoors and enjoy the comforts of home and human companionship.

What to Do About Frustration Barking

Frustration barking is very painful to listen to because you know it means a dog is in real trouble. But it is the simplest to cure:

- Remove the dog from the situation that is causing the frustration. Take him inside, let him be together with you, be part of the family.

- Give him something to do—it usually doesn't need to be much. Take him with you in the car when you go places. Go for a little walk now and then, with opportunities for the dog to sniff and explore. Maybe have him search for some treats you throw around your garden.

That is usually all it takes. The most important thing for a dog is to be a part of the family. That means being together with the family and going places with them. Even sitting in the car when you shop, as long as he is not left alone too long, can be companionship to the dog. If you also let him have the chance of using his senses by sniffing and exploring, he will get the mental stimulation he needs.

It should be possible for anyone to do this, and thereby let your dog have a good life. If you cannot do as much as this, you probably should not have a dog at all. He needs you.

Spending time with your dog, involving him in activities as simple as a daily walk, will go a long way toward relieving frustration your dog might otherwise experience.

Summing Up Frustration Barking

Frustration barking is the kind of barking that will start to occur when a dog becomes so desperate and frustrated over a long period of time that he starts adopting behaviors that will help him cope with the situation. Barking is one of these behaviors, but you should also watch out for others. Chewing inappropriate objects is another one. Eating rocks or licking himself until he bleeds are other common examples.

The sound of frustration barking is typically a long series of endless static (same tone repeated over and over) barking. If he stops barking temporarily he will usually be very still, showing no movement or maybe a little restless wandering.

This kind of barking can, of course, not be punished. Change his environment, let him have a life.

8   Learned Barking

Learned barking often starts out as one of the other kinds of barking mentioned above. What makes it distinct is that the owner has usually—consciously or unconsciously—somehow reinforced the behavior. Usually this is unintentional, but not always.

How it sounds and activity involved. This type of barking is very easy to recognize when you know what to look for. The dog barks, takes a break, and looks around. He is actually seeking attention or whatever reinforcement he has received in the past for barking. If the attention or reinforcement is not forthcoming, he will start barking again, seeking the "reward" that is usually given to him by someone who is nearby, most often his owner.

Should you reprimand this? Punishing this behavior will not work. In the first place it will give the dog more attention, and therefore the established behavior will continue if the dog finds attention rewarding as most do. The better solution is to teach the dog another behavior instead. If something is learned, it can be unlearned, but it should be done in such a way that the dog doesn't get any negative associations. And hopefully he will learn something appropriate that will last.

What can we do about this? If you see that you have a barking problem that most likely was learned, then you have to do two things:

1. For a period of time—maybe one month as a start, sometimes a little longer—your job will be to make sure that the dog does not get a chance to do the unwanted behavior. You want to take away the possibility he will react by barking using management techniques. That means not leaving the dog alone out in the garden, not standing for

a long time chatting with anyone, or anything else that might cause the dog to bark for attention.

2. Start training, but the training used will vary depending on what kind of learned barking is involved. Remember, learned barking has usually been reinforced by the owner, even if the owner is not aware of it. You need to identify the triggering event, then train the dog to have a different response than barking.

Training Techniques

Let's look at some of the training programs you can use. I will give you some recipes that can be a great help. Just remember to be systematic in your training. Do not go so fast that the dog can't figure out what you want him to do, reward for the right behavior, and be clear. If you do, the dog will learn fast. Sometimes, amazingly so.

To begin, start by teaching the dog the hand signal mentioned earlier. Your hand can be a visual aid to make the dog stop barking (or something else), or just not start some other behavior at all. This can be a great help in all your training. You can do it in several ways:

- No matter what kind of training you do, when you finish up, hold up the palm of your hand, and just turn away from the dog.

- He will learn very quickly that the hand signal means you are finished and to stop whatever it is you were doing. Do not say anything, just use the hand signal and then turn away.

- If your dog is begging for food or attention, do the same thing: hold up your hand and then turn/look away. Say nothing.

- If you want to get up and go into another room, use your hand signal, then leave. Come back and sit down without giving the dog any attention.

- Use your hand signal when you need to leave your dog in the house or in the car for awhile. The dog usually gets the point very quickly.

The method is effective with other animals as well—I have used it with horses and cats, achieving the same result. I always had to lead the worst and most excitable horses in and out of the stable, and because I used the hand signal they went along much more willingly with me.

Let us look specifically at some other situations where the dog may have learned to bark.

Teach the Dog to be Quiet When You Stop to Talk with People

Dogs frequently bark when you encounter another person on a walk or in other situations. The dog barks and receives attention from either you or the other person—essentially he has learned to bark in this situation and has been rewarded for it.

You will need a helper in this exercise and you should teach your dog the hand signal described above.

1. Walk your dog on a loose leash, calmly and slowly. Have your helper walk toward you.

2. As you approach and then begin to pass by each other, make sure you walk in a curving path as much as necessary while passing. You should be between your dog and the helper as you start to pass each other.

3. Now approach each other again, this time taking a smaller curve. If the dog shows an interest in walking towards the other person, use the hand signal with the dog, and then step in between the dog and the helper to form a bit of a barrier.

4. When you can pass closely by the helper without incident, take the next step and stop near the helper—but only for a second! Then continue walking. Keep using the hand signal at this stage and in each one that follows.

5. Next, turn around, stop for a second and say "hello." Then walk on.

6. Next time, stop and say "hello," and shake hands, then walk on.

Continue to increase the time you stop and talk to the helper, remembering to use the hand signal. After a few sessions you can stop when you meet somebody, chat a little—not too long in the beginning—and walk on. If you stand too long and the dog gets restless, use the hand signal, wait a few seconds, and walk on. While the dog is quiet!

When Your Dog Barks at Guests

This is a common example of learned barking. Guests come into your home, the dog barks, and then gets lots of attention for doing so. (See a related example in Chapter 3, Excitement Barking.)

- When a guest arrives, put the dog on a loose leash, making sure you do not pull or hold him tight. Keep your hands passive, but hold back if he pulls.

- Sit down as far away from the guest as possible, placing yourself between the dog and the guest.

- Ignore the dog, just continue to hold the leash so he cannot approach the guest. Use the hand signal without looking at the dog.

- The dog will calm down once he knows he cannot approach. Dogs are smart—they will give up when they realize they can't do something.

- When the dog begins to relax and has maintained some calm for a while, take off the leash. If he gets up to go to the guest, let him do it, but instruct the guest not to interact with the dog in any way.

- Tell the guest to let you know when he wants to get up so you can put the dog on leash again. Only then should the guest get up.

It does not take many training sessions before the dog relaxes around guests.

Barking in the Car

Learned barking in the car can occur for a variety of reasons, ranging from the dog being excited about going somewhere fun (arriving at a fun place is rewarding) to unease due to a previous experience with car-sickness. For some people this is the most irritating barking they experience and I can understand that because you have to concentrate while driving, and of course it can be dangerous if you don't. It doesn't help to become angry, yell or scream at the dog—you need to keep cool and try to find a solution. But finding a solution requires you to figure out what it is that is causing the barking.

Car-sickness. Many puppies get car-sick, just like kids, because their balance system is not fully developed. They cannot help this, and it will pass as they grow older. To avoid the problem, you should drive only very short distances with a puppy until he is at least 6 months old. After that point the issues with the balance systems are usually over.

If your puppy does experience car-sickness, he may begin to feel sick just at the sight of the car because he remembers the terrible unpleasantness. This may also cause negative associations with other dogs and your veterinarian because the driving trips are often made to go to training classes and vets. Try to avoid long drives and use car-sickness medicine if necessary.

If the dog has learned that going in the car means he will feel sick, he will develop negative associations with it. Your training needs to focus on changing the dog's association by:

- Take only very short trips so he doesn't have enough time to become sick.

- Drive only to very pleasant places or events—for a walk, meeting friends, visiting a dog park, or other things the dog enjoys.

- Sometimes it helps to have the dog sit on the floor beside the driver seat. The movements of the car are much worse the further back you get. I tested it out, and sitting in the rear of a long car made me sick right away!

Excitement. If the reason for the barking is excitement because the dog has learned that every time you go in the car you go to some place interesting and fun, then see the suggested training in the Excitement Barking section.

To illustrate this further, I was once working with an adult dog who was as nice and lovely as can be, but he barked in the car. He was a smart dog, so I planned an intensive training session for him. I went to the little village nearby, and drove up and down the main street. I stopped at every shop, meaning we would drive for about five meters, then get out and go into a shop, and then come back out again. By the time we had stopped and started up several times, he stopped barking—and he never did it again. I made sure that he went with me in the car a lot, mostly to dull places where nothing eventful happened.

Dogs bark in cars for a variety of reasons.

Barking for Attention

A dog is out in the garden or a kennel alone and starts barking at the sight of something. Observing the dog from the house behind a curtain you might see:

- The dog barks a few times, and then turns around looking towards his owner. He waits for someone to yell at him—as has happened in the past. If there is no response, he repeats the pattern to see if anybody is listening.

- The dog has probably learned that his owner will talk to him and ask him to stop. Of course he stopped while being talked to—but he also learned that he gets attention when he barks. In other words he didn't learn not to bark because barking got attention from his owner.

This dog barks a couple times, and then turns toward his owner looking for attention.

Barking When Encountering Other Dogs

A woman came to me because her dog always barked at other dogs when out on walks. She thought he was "aggressive." We went out to a nearby field, and I had an assistant with another dog approach the woman and her dog. Here is what happened:

- The dog started to bark, moved forward in a lunging movement, barked a couple more times, and then turned toward the owner, seeking her "appreciation."

- I instructed the owner to do nothing when this happened, and look away if the dog turned to look at her. When he barked and turned the next time without getting attention, the dog looked a bit bewildered, went back to barking at the other dog, but this time only half heartedly. When the dog turned towards the owner again, going all the way up to her, pushing his nose at her. He was very clearly saying "why don't you say anything, didn't you hear how wonderful I was in barking at that dog?"

This is a very typical learned behavior. The dog had been given attention—and in the dog's mind rewarded—so the barking, in this instance, had become a learned behavior.

The "aggressive" dog moved forward and barked at the other dog, then quickly turned toward his owner looking for reinforcement.

Barking When the Doorbell Rings

I was called to someone's home because they had a guarding problem. We sat talking in the living room when the doorbell rang. The dog got up, barked a little but not very enthusiastically, and then turned to the owners for "support." This was so obviously a learned behavior that it could not have been clearer. No guarding, no aggression—but he had been given attention in the past for this behavior, attention which the dog found rewarding in some way. This can include:

- Talking to the dog.

- Touching and petting the dog.

- Giving the dog a command to sit, lie down, or something else.

- Being taken out of the room and into another.

- Getting a reward when the barking stops.

- Looking at the dog.

Even subtle attention given to a dog can help reinforce his barking when guests arrive.

Barking Due to Unintentional Training

Several years ago I was very busy, my telephones were ringing all day. I also had four dogs, and sometimes I had to quickly take them out in the short amount of time between calls. Eventually my normally quiet dogs all started to bark the moment I put down the receiver, or rather when I said "goodbye."

It took me awhile before I was able to figure it out. Apparently I had been consistently rushing out with them right after having said "goodbye" on the phone. They had learned that "goodbye" meant going out for a walk, which, like most dogs, they found very exciting. But I had also taught them to bark.

Well, obviously I had to do some training, but it didn't take long before we were back to normal. I had to be a bit more careful about how I did things in the future. This was a good learning experience for me. It is so easy to teach dogs things without intending to, and it can happen so quickly.

Barking When You Stop to Greet Someone

The same thing can happen when you are out walking, and then stop to talk to someone. The dog starts to fuss. He whines, scratches, and then starts to bark. You feel embarrassed, so you get on with your walk—and the dog has learned to make a fuss to get you walking again.

There are many other situations in which this happens. It can be quite fun to see what dogs learn when we are not conscious about the results of our own actions. Look at yourself—I am sure you can find your own examples.

Try not to reward your dog for barking and fussing, such as when you stop to visit with a friend.

Acknowledging your dog in any way is rewarding to him. Do not look at him or bend toward him as this lady does.

Summing Up Learned Barking

Dogs bark in certain situations due to a variety of reasons (excitement, fear, etc.). Learned barking in these situations occurs when the owner or someone else inadvertently reinforces the barking behavior. It is usually easy to recognize learned barking because the dog will bark, stop and look around, and then bark again, seeking attention.

The keys to dealing with learned barking are to recognize what is triggering the barking and train an alternative reaction that does not involve barking. Make sure you do not continue to "reward" this kind of barking.

9 Breed Related Barking and Other Vocal Expressions

Ever since people have been living with dogs, they have bred them for the skills they wanted or desired. If they needed fast dogs for hunting, they would pick out the dogs that ran the fastest to breed. If they needed guard dogs, they would look for dogs with the strongest guarding behaviors and breed them. And if they wanted barking, that is what they would breed for.

There is a lot of interesting history relating to specific breeds. The Great Dane, looked upon as calmness itself, was bred for its unique ability to jump high. There was a desire in Medieval times for dogs to run ahead of hunters riding horses and then jump up high onto the back of large prey like elk and moose. This action would knock the prey down making it easier for the hunters to kill them. If you see a young Great Dane today, you might see the genetic disposition they have for these enormous jumps! When they get excited, they can jump as high as six feet straight up from a standing start.

Breed Related Barking

In the scattered farms throughout Europe and other places with lots of space and few people, early settlers preferred dogs who barked when strangers were approaching as a warning. Today, if you get a dog like a Great Pyrenees, you will find out that they still are very good at barking in similar situations. They are genetically dispositioned to do it and it would be cruel to punish them for it. Some hunting dogs, like Beagles, are bred to track rabbits and to bark in short intervals so that the hunters can hear where they are. I live in an area where there are lots of dogs bred to do this. During hunting season I can hear them in the hills behind me and can easily follow their trail. For hunters, this kind of barking is important, making it so much easier to know where the dog and prey are.

From this it can be seen that many dogs have been bred to perform a certain kind of bark, because it was helpful, necessary, and valued. This breeding has been going on for thousands of years compared to the relatively short time we have kept dogs as pets only—not enough time for this behavior to change. Icelandic dogs, rabbit hunters, and herding dogs all still bark a lot.

Interestingly, there are dogs who do not bark much, most of whom have to run fast during the performance of their "job." It is not easy or efficient to bark while using a lot of energy on running. Try it yourself! So racing hounds like Greyhounds and Whippets tend to bark less than many breeds. The Husky or Greenland dog, both of whom have to spend all their energy on long sledding trips, also tend to bark less.

Know what barking characteristics have been bred into the kind of dog you choose.

If you are getting a dog, always learn something first about the breed's characteristics, especially things like barking and guarding behaviors. Our forefathers did a good job in picking out useful dogs with a purpose, and it will make it easier for the dog and for you if you do not choose the completely wrong breed.

If you live close to a school or a field where they play basketball or soccer or where there are young people running around all the time, you especially should not choose a breed who alerts quickly by barking. It could cause you a lot of problems. You might be able to manage the situation, but be aware of all the work you will need to devote to the situation. While you might be able to tolerate it, think about other people who might get irritable and nervous because of the barking. Think about such things when you are planning to get a dog. Maybe you will choose another breed then—remember there are so many to choose from.

Other Vocal Expressions
Howling

Howling is used more among wolves than among dogs, but dogs can also howl and do it in certain situations.

Howling can mean different things, including:

"Here I am—where are you?" A common example is when the sled-dogs in my area start howling on the top of the hill, and other sled dogs living on nearby hilltops answer. This back and forth howling can go on for a long time.

Gathering of the pack. My male collie used to howl when the two young "girls" in his pack took a trip up the hill behind us to meet their moose friends. If he thought they were up there too long, he called them home by howling, and they always came right back.

I need you! A typical example of this is the lonely dog calling for someone to come—whether he has been left too long at home alone, or out in a kennel, or tied up. It can also be a male calling for a female in heat. Many people hear their male dogs howling, and it usually means a female is in heat nearby. If he cannot go to her, he calls her to come to him.

In search of their own kind. If you go up on a hilltop and start howling, you will likely hear howls from other dogs or wolves. Canines cannot help answering howls, whether from people, ambulance sirens, train whistles, and other similar sounds.

Even indoors, dogs may howl in response to other dogs or similar sounds like sirens.

I'm lonely. Dogs will howl when they are lonely. They howl instinctively because they think howling will cause someone to come to them—and they can get terrified when it does not happen. When a dog is howling he is often calling for help, for someone to save him.

Whining

Newborn puppies whine to orient themselves toward their mother, and to encourage her to move closer to them. When you take a puppy home and he whines, that is essentially what he is doing—calling for his mom, who is suddenly gone. This time when mum doesn't come, it will be a shock to him, and he should not have that shock. He needs mom, and you take mom's place as long as he needs you. A puppy grows up fast and will become independent, but for the puppy's mental health you must give him security in the beginning.

Puppies often whine after being separated from their mothers.

Dogs who whine also do so because they are hungry, thirsty, need to relieve themselves, or are afraid. This is, of course, the same as with puppies—they are seeking help from someone.

Adult dogs can sometimes learn to whine because they get attention for it. We have a tendency to hush a dog who is whining to keep him quiet, especially when talking with somebody, or watching a favorite program on television. The dog very quickly learns that he gets attention for whining, and can become really good at using it.

Dogs can also whine when they are excited about something. You should look at it the same way as you do excitement barking (see Chapter 3).

Growling

Growling is frightening to many people who don't see it for what it really is: a message, an expression that communicates the dog is experiencing some difficulty. Something scary, threatening, painful, or whatever it is at the moment. It can mean:

- Don't come closer—I don't like it.

- This hurts.

- I can't take anymore of this.

- Don't take my food, I am hungry.

- I have had enough, please stop.

Growling is probably the most misunderstood of all canine vocal expressions. Too many dogs have been put down for wrong and unfair reasons because people misunderstand the meaning behind growls.

I am never afraid of growling. You should view it as a clear message about how the dog is feeling. It is up to you to solve whatever the dog is finding conflicting and help the dog to cope. Recognize that growling happens when the dog is starting to feel real bad, and it is important to respect that, and do not let it come to the point where the dog feels he must defend himself.

Growling may be scary, but the dog is letting you know how he feels so you can take action before he resorts to a bite. It is a nice and clear way to let you know how he feels. He also turns his head to show you he really doesn't mean any harm—if you do not push it.

If you punish away the growl to an extent that the dog doesn't dare to use it as a warning, you can be in big trouble. The next time the dog would have used it he won't, and he may feel he has no choice but to bite.

Accept the growl as a great way of understanding how the dog is feeling about something.

10   Final Thoughts

We have reviewed the many different types of barking dogs engage in and how to manage/train to avoid problem barking. Whatever the cause, the basic recipe for solving problem barking follows these steps:

1. First you have to figure out what kind of barking your dog is expressing. It can be one of the barking types we have described here, or it can be a mixture of two to three different types. A dog can have mixed feelings. He can be excited and a little unsure at the same time. He can be afraid and defensive. Combinations of these often go together, and barking can involve more than one emotion.

2. Make notes on what the situation is (such as time of day, being outdoors, guest arriving) when the dog barks and observe the dog's actions.

3. If you suspect that the dog has a chronic stress problem, you have to find out what is causing it so you can start reducing it. Stress comes most often from the environment and can have its roots in what we do with the dog, how we do it, but also can be related to pain and illness.

Once you have analyzed the situation, you can determine what to do about it. These include:

- Stop doing things that you think are making the dog react by barking.

- Better management techniques to avoid exposing the dog to things he reacts badly to.

- Implement training techniques, especially to counter the negative associations the dog may have formed.

- Changing routines and changing your attitude about the dog.

- Using medication, preferably alternative medication for things like car-sickness.

- Take responsibility away from the dog so he does not feel the desire to guard or defend himself against a real or perceived threat (the placing yourself between the dog and the threat technique).

- Help your dog to avoid difficult situations.

- Be sure nobody is scaring your dog.

Whatever you do to solve barking related problems:

1. You must accept that your dog should be allowed to bark sometimes. It is natural. He has a voice, and needs to be allowed to use it.

2. The recipe for solving problems involves taking away (or at least reducing) the possibility that the dog will feel the need to react by barking and if he does, teach the dog a new alternative behavior in its place.

Keep in Mind

Barking is self rewarding, and therefore we cannot ignore barking to get rid of it. In a few cases, we have to ignore barking in a specific situation, but only over the short run. Over the long run, we have to avoid letting the dog get into the situations where he feels the need to bark.

It is futile to reward a dog for being quiet right after having barked. There are two reasons for it:

- Dogs learn well by backward chaining, and will quickly learn to: bark, then stop barking, and then get a reward. Dogs learn a lot of things exactly this way.

- Dogs learn best when getting a reward for something physical they have done. Rewarding for absolutely nothing (i.e., not barking) will not lead to learning, just frustration.

I have done some related tests on people. In my trainer classes, I have them experience things to be able to understand how a dog might feel about the same event. When they are all sitting quietly, maybe just listening, or thinking about a problem, I suddenly stop by a student and praise him. Having assured myself that the student is not doing anything at the moment, the student becomes completely bewildered, and does not understand what the praise is for. They all say that they feel totally frustrated, and find it unpleasant.

Sometimes I try being "angry" at one of them (they have all been warned before I do it!). They never understand why I am reprimanding them. I can get angry when a student raises his hand, fiddles with a pencil, scratches his nose, or something else. Even though they are warned about it, it feels very unpleasant, and the student will feel uncertain a long time afterward. And they never have a clue as to what I was "angry" about. Maybe we should think more about what we actually say and do to our dog to understand the reactions we get.

🐾 Distraction is a frequently used technique with barking—but it can actually be a direct reward for the unwanted behavior because distraction may equal attention in the dog's mind. By offering a distraction to the dog, even using a harsh voice—we are rewarding the dog directly for the unwanted behavior. And the attention helps the dog learn to do it more, more intensely, and more often, whether the behavior is barking or something else.

There is one kind of distraction you can use. It is very effective with puppies, young dogs, and curious dogs. Move away from the dog, turn your back on him, and find something that makes a rattling sound or at least something that makes the dog curious. The dog gets no reward or attention, he just gets distracted from the situation. Pretend to be interested in the object when the dog comes up to you, but do not talk to the dog for maybe 5 seconds, to avoid any kind of backward chaining! Dogs are curious by nature—if they are allowed to be—and that provides us a lot of wonderful opportunities to trick the dog when it is necessary.

🐾 "Time-outs" can be very effective, but not if you go to a barking dog and bring him out of a room, for instance. That is attention, and therefore a reward. You need to leave the dog alone, closing the door behind you without even looking at the dog if a "time-out" is going to be used effectively.

Summing Up

🐾 Barking is the way dogs express an emotion of some kind. In order to be able to reduce it, we need to know why the dog is barking. There are different ways of dealing with barking, depending on the cause of the barking.

🐾 If you have read the entire book, you will see that it is completely ineffective to punish a dog for barking, no matter what kind of barking you are dealing with. At best the dog will not learn anything, and in the worst case it can have serious consequences.

🐾 Accept that dogs bark as a part of their natural communication with others—there is no point in trying to stop it completely. We only need to do something when it becomes unnatural and a problem.

🐾 Barking means something, the dog is trying to tell you something, so use your knowledge and understanding to find out what it is.

🐾 When you think you understand why the dog is barking, make a plan for how to deal with it.

🐾 Physiologically humans are not very different from other mammals, even if we want to be. Emotionally we are not so different either. We all have a limbic system and that means we all have the same emotions. We fear things, so do dogs. We are frightened of threats, anger, pain, and noise. So are dogs. We get angry when we are being pestered, pushed to do things we cannot cope with. So do dogs. How we react might be slightly different from species to species, but a lot of it is the same. It has all to do with survival.

🐾 Animals have feelings and emotions. When things happen to them, they react with emotions be it sorrow, anger, happiness, fear. There are still people who think that animals do not have feelings and emotions. Of course they have. They have the same nerve system and the same limbic system. Stress works exactly the same way as with us creating similar problems. All you have to do is look at an animal to see the emotions in his face, eyes, and body posture. It is all very clear if we just bother to observe and understand.

🐾 We cannot let our human arrogance deprive animals of their emotions. We must learn to see them and respect them. We can, if we want to. We must, if we want to be human.

Recommended Reading

These and other great books are available at www.dogwise.com:

Roger Abrantes, *Evolution of Canine Social Behavior*

Brenda Aloff, *Canine Body Language: A Photographic Guide*

Marc Bekoff, *Minding Animals: Awareness, Emotions, and Heart*

Jean Donaldson, *The Culture Clash*

Barry Eaton, *Dominance: Fact or Fiction?*

Cindy Engel, *Wild Health: Lessons in Natural Wellness from the Animal Kingdom*

Jeffrey Masson, *When Elephants Weep*

Jeffrey Masson, *Dogs Never Lie About Love*

James O'Heare, *Canine Separation Anxiety Workbook*

Turid Rugaas, *On Talking Terms With Dogs*

Turid Rugaas, *My Dog Pulls, What Do I Do?*

Turid Rugaas, *Calming Signals: What Your Dog Tells You*, DVD

Terry Ryan, *The Bark Stops Here*

Nicole Wilde, *It's Not the Dogs, It's the People!*

About the Author

Turid Rugaas is one of the most influential dog behaviorists in the world due to her ground-breaking work on canine calming signals. A former racehorse trainer, she has spent most of her life with animals with whom she clearly has a special bond. She is founder of Hagen Hundeskole in Norway, where she trains other trainers, dogs, and their owners. Turid is much in demand around the world so she is frequently traveling to deliver lectures and seminars. She also is a founding member of the Pet Dog Trainers of Europe, an organization devoted to teaching through kindness and respect. She is the author of *On Talking Terms With Dogs: Calming Signals* (both book and dvd formats) and *My Dog Pulls: What Do I Do?* Turid can be reached at turidrug@frisurf.no or Box 109, 3360 Geithus Norway.

Also available from Dogwise Publishing

Go to dogwise.com for more books and ebooks.

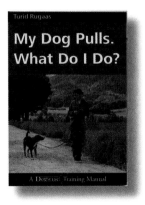

My Dog Pulls

What Do I Do?

Turid Rugaas

Wouldn't it be great if your dog walked politely on a leash instead of making it a tug-of-war? From Norwegian dog trainer Turid Rugaas, it's easy to learn and works on any age, size or breed of dog.

On Talking Terms with Dogs:

Calming Signals

Turid Rugaas

Norwegian dog trainer Turid Rugaas taught the world that humans cannot only learn to read canine body language but use their own body language to communicate with dogs. One of the most influential books on dog behavior today.

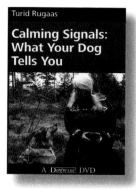

Calming Signals DVD

Calming Signals

Turid Rugaas

Learn how dogs' facial expressions and body postures can communicate information to other dogs and to humans. In this DVD you can clearly see "calming signals" in action.

The Canine Kingdom of Scent

Fun Activities Using Your Dog's Natural Instincts

Anne Lill Kvam

You've seen your dog's incredible sense of smell in action, hoovering up crumbs in the kitchen and on walks. But do you know that you can use it for training, mental stimulation and bonding? Follow the steps here and succeed.

Dogwise.com is your source for quality books, ebooks, DVDs, training tools and treats.

We've been selling to the dog fancier for more than 25 years and we carefully screen our products for quality information, safety, durability and FUN! You'll find something for every level of dog enthusiast on our website www.dogwise.com or drop by our store in Wenatchee, Washington.